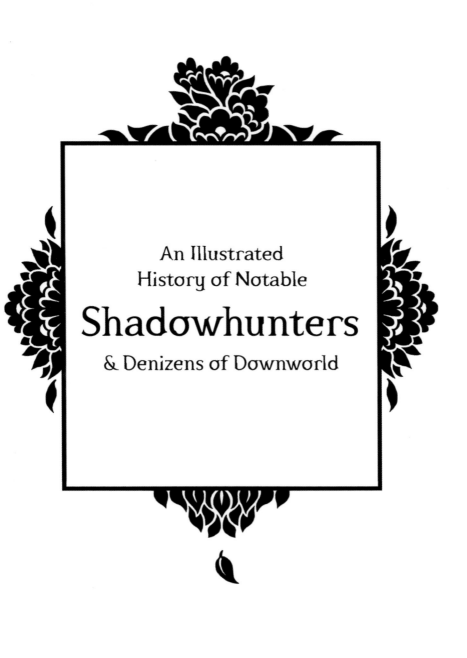

An Illustrated
History of Notable

Shadowhunters

& Denizens of Downworld

An Illustrated
History of Notable

Shadowhunters

& Denizens of Downworld

CASSANDRA CLARE

ILLUSTRATED BY
CASSANDRA JEAN

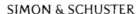

SIMON & SCHUSTER

First published in Great Britain in 2016 by Simon and Schuster UK Ltd
A CBS COMPANY

First published in the USA in 2016 by TopatoCo Books, Easthampton, MA.

7 9 10 8 6

Simon & Schuster UK Ltd
1st Floor, 222 Gray's Inn Road
London WC1X 8HB

www.simonandschuster.co.uk

Simon & Schuster Australia, Sydney
Simon & Schuster India, New Delhi

A CIP catalogue record for this book is available from the British Library.

HB ISBN 978-1-4711-6119-3
TPB ISBN 978-1-4711-6120-9
eBook ISBN 978-1-4711-6121-6

Printed and bound in China

Contents

The Infernal Devices

Alexei de Quincey

Born Unknown
Species Vampire
Favorite weapon Teeth

De Quincey was the head of the London vampire clan in the late Victorian period. When the Shadowhunters of the London Enclave raided de Quincey's hideout in Chelsea, they came across very unpleasant wallpaper. De Quincey had commissioned an elaborate design involving hundreds of screaming humans, writhing on a blood-red background.

Alexei de Quincey

Venus Flytrap 🌸 Deceit

Axel Mortmain (Hollingworth Shade)

Born 1803
Species Mundane human
Favorite weapon Automaton army

Mortmain had an unusual upbringing, for he was adopted and raised by two warlocks, John and Anne Shade. He gained his love of the mechanical from John, who was fascinated by the possibilities of combining magic with clockwork. After Axel's death, the Clave searched his properties. At his residence they found a hidden room filled entirely with music boxes. It is not known whether they were created by John, Axel, or another person entirely. None had magical properties. All of them were well cared for, and had been frequently used.

Axel Mortmain

Red Clover ❖ King of Industry

Benedict Lightwood

Born 1831
Species Nephilim
Favorite weapon Blades
Family Lightwood, Unknown

A s a young boy, Benedict was fascinated by reptiles. During disagreements with his father, which were frequent, Benedict would flee into the countryside to search for frogs, turtles, and whatever other creatures he could find. He was especially fond of snakes.

Benedict Lightwood

Tuberose ❧ Dangerous Pleasures

Cecily Herondale

Born 1863
Species Nephilim
Married name Lightwood
Favorite weapon Blades
Family Herondale

Even before training as a Shadowhunter, Cecily had uncommonly good aim. The Herondale children would make a game of throwing rocks to knock objects like pinecones and empty kitchen canisters off of fence posts, and Cecily annoyed her older siblings greatly with her innate skill.

Cecily Herondale

Periwinkle — *Tender Recollections*

Charlotte Branwell

Born 1855
Species Nephilim
Maiden name Fairchild
Favorite weapon Sword
Family Fairchild, Unknown

Charlotte and her father Granville Fairchild did not always see eye to eye, but there was one place in which they always enjoyed each other's company: at the chessboard. Granville taught his daughter to play when she was seven years old, and the game afforded them an opportunity to spend time together over the course of many years.

Charlotte Branwell

Wild Plum ❧❧❧ Independence

Dark Sisters

Born Unknown
Species Warlock, Demon
Favorite weapon Spells

L ittle is known of the history of the Dark Sisters, who terrified London in the 1870s, yet their strong connection with each other was undeniable. Records of two women sounding very much like them have been found dating back to the 1600s, when the sisters were forced into seclusion by witch hunts. It is unknown why Mrs. Dark, a demon, chose to spend so much time in a dangerous part of the human world. Possibly it was because she could not bring her sister with her to the demon realms.

The Dark Sisters

Black Rainflower ∞ Hatred

Edmund Herondale

Born 1835
Species Nephilim (exiled)
Favorite weapon n/a
Family Herondale, Unknown

Edmund Herondale left the Shadowhunter world as a young man, but his children, Will and Cecily Herondale, chose to step back into that world. To Edmund's delight, his son and daughter and their families found ways to visit around the holidays every year. Their appearance was cause for much merry-making, and Edmund would make a point of baking gingerbread, his one specialty, when they arrived.

Edmund Herondale

Mourning Bride Flower ~ 'I have lost all'

Gabriel Lightwood

Born 1860
Species Nephilim
Favorite weapon Seraph blade
Family Lightwood, Pangborn

Gabriel was not particularly close with his father. After his brother Gideon Lightwood moved to Spain, Gabriel was rather lonely. He read his way through the library, learned to identify the plants in the gardens, and even briefly considered learning topiary. It was at this critical juncture that Benedict Lightwood became suddenly interested in his younger son, inviting Gabriel to accompany him on Shadowhunter business and holding court in his study late into the night, telling Gabriel stories of their glorious family history. Regrettably, many of these stories were completely made up, or drastically altered from their true form to fit Benedict's purposes.

Gabriel Lightwood

Delphinium ⬥ Haughtiness

Gideon Lightwood

Born 1858
Species Nephilim
Favorite weapon Seraph blade
Family Lightwood, Pangborn

Once held in the sway of his father, Gideon Lightwood's life changed dramatically when he spent a year in Spain. Gideon was delighted by the warmth of his hosts, and their kindness gave him a new perspective on his upbringing. He longed for his brother Gabriel Lightwood to share in the experience with him, and resolved to make changes to their lives when he returned home.

Gideon Lightwood

Stock ∽ *You will always be Beautiful to me*

Henry Branwell

Born 1856
Species Nephilim
Favorite weapon Varied, all invented
by Henry himself
Family Branwell, Unknown

H enry was an inventor from the time he was small. His parents were alternately amused and frustrated by his desire to redesign common household appliances. After a particularly frightening incident with a wringer mangle, Henry was encouraged to turn his creativity to mechanical pursuits that were not related to household chores. This inadvertently steered him towards the boundary-breaking work that eventually made him famous.

Henry Branwell

Clematis ⚬⟋⟍⟋⟍⟋⟍⟋⟍⟋⟍⟋⟍ *Ingenuity*

Jem Carstairs

Born 1861
Species Nephilim
Favorite weapon Sword
Family Carstairs, Ke

J em's journey back to himself when he left the Silent Brothers was not an easy one. Unsure how to process the years he had spent in a distant emotional and physical state, Jem eventually turned to music. At first his ability to play the violin was nowhere near what it had been before he joined the Gregori, but that was acceptable. Jem wasn't aiming for technical skill. He was aiming for a nonverbal way to express what he had lost and what he had gained, and he found it.

Jem Carstairs

White Zinnia ⚜ Goodness

Jessamine Lovelace

Born 1860
Species Nephilim
Married name Gray
Favorite weapon Parasol
Family Lovelace, Unknown

Jessamine's ghost guarded the London Institute for many decades, but her behavior wasn't always benevolent. If she disapproved of a resident's fashion choices, they might find the offending articles missing, sometimes replaced by clothing that Jessamine deemed worthy. Since she had no way to leave the Institute, these garments were borrowed from other residents, causing much confusion.

Jessamine Lovelace Gray

Bay Leaf ∽ I Change but in Death

Linette Owens

Born 1839
Species Mundane human
Married name Herondale

When Linette's children, Will and Cecily Herondale, would bring their families to visit at holiday times, Linette was fond of corralling everyone into games. Charades and Pass the Slipper were favorites. Forfeits was popular among the children, but usually led to fights between Will and Gabriel Lightwood. Linette tried to steer the family away from games involving wagers, because of her husband Edmund's nearly ruinous penchant for gambling.

Linette Herondale

Cinquefoil ♥ Maternal Affection

Nathaniel Gray

Born 1859
Species Mundane human
Favorite weapon Deceit

As a child, Nate Gray was briefly interested in sketching. It was a relatively low-cost hobby for the cash-strapped Gray family, and they used scrap paper whenever they could get it. While he had talent, Nate was frustrated by his inability to convey the images exactly how he saw them in his mind's eye. He became belligerent and short-tempered about practicing. His sister, Tessa Gray, and their guardian Harriet Moore were both relieved when he gave up the hobby.

Nathaniel Gray

Columbine ⸎ Folly

Sophie Collins

Born 1858
Species Nephilim (Ascendant)
Married name Lightwood
Favorite weapon Hand mirror
Family Ashdown

As a child growing up with the Sight, Sophie Collins had an unusual perspective on London. From the time she was young she was drawn to places where the two worlds she witnessed drew close to each other; carnivals, solstice celebrations, Westminster Abbey. Sadly, her wanderings were limited by her need for employment.

Sophie Collins

Blue Bells ❦ Gratitude

Tatiana Blackthorn

Born 1862
Species Nephilim
Maiden name Lightwood
Favorite weapon n/a
Family Lightwood, Pangborn

T atiana had very little time with her mother, Barbara Lightwood, for the latter died tragically when Tatiana was only a baby. As a young girl Tatiana became prone to fits of inarticulate rage, blaming her mother's absence on her brothers, Gabriel and Gideon Lightwood. Tatiana felt she had been cheated, and was extremely jealous of the time her brothers had spent with their mother. Her feelings of rage only intensified when her father was transformed into a giant worm that devoured her fiancé in front of her.

Tatiana Blackthorn

Orange Lily ⚜ *Passionate Hate*

Tessa Gray

Born 1862
Species Warlock/Nephilim
Married names Herondale, Carstairs
Favorite weapon Shapeshifting
Family Starkweather

Tessa lived in Paris for ten years. For the first five she shared a flat with the warlock Magnus Bane. The two developed several shared routines; Sunday Morning Tea and Pastries, Friday Night Dancing, Saturday Sightseeing, and Wednesday Sipping Chocolate, but eventually Tessa found that Magnus's flamboyant lifestyle did not agree with her. She took her own room in a peaceful garret, lining the walls with books.

Tessa Gray

Red Verbena ∽ ~ *United with Love Against Evil*

William Owen Herondale

Born 1861
Species Nephilim
Favorite weapon Dagger
Family Herondale

When Will and his parabatai Jem Carstairs were twelve years old, they made a game of playing on the roof of the Institute. They kept this pastime secret as long as possible, until Charlotte Branwell eventually caught them at it. After that, they had to wait until Henry and Charlotte were out on Institute business to continue their game.

Will is famous among Shadowhunters for his heroism and his crippling fear of ducks.

Will Herondale

Love lies Bleeding ❧ Hopeless Love

Woolsey Marmaduke Scott

Born Unknown
Species Werewolf
Favorite weapon Biting wit

Woolsey founded the Praetor Lupus to honor the brother who raised him, Ralf Scott, who was killed by vampires. The organization's mission to help newly turned and struggling Downworlders was in marked contrast to Woolsey's flippant style, but he was serious about creating an institution that would last. Woolsey credits his brother Ralf for giving him the space to become his own person, even though the two brothers had wildly different attitudes and ambitions. Ralf always encouraged his younger brother to follow his own path, and Woolsey was grateful to be able to make his brother's wishes into reality.

Woolsey Scott

Begonia ❦ *Fanciful Nature*

The Last Hours

Alastair Carstairs

Born 1884
Species Nephilim
Favorite weapon Cortana
Family Carstairs, Turan

Alastair and his sister Cordelia didn't have much in common, but in childhood they did share an early interest in architecture. Inspired by their last name, the two collaborated on building elaborate castles out of wooden blocks.

Alastair Carstairs

Currant ❧ Thy Frown will Kill me

Anna Lightwood

Born 1884
Species Nephilim
Favorite weapon Wit
Family Lightwood, Herondale

Anna Lightwood has always had a knack for making people feel special. Even when she was young, she had a habit of finding the child least at ease and making them comfortable. Her tea parties under tables, tree climbing expeditions, and hide-and-go-seek adventures were much anticipated by her cousins, as were, in later years, her fashion choices.

Anna Lightwood

Maidenhair Fern ❦ Secrecy

Charles Buford Fairchild

Born 1879
Species Nephilim
Favorite weapon Diplomacy
Family Fairchild, Branwell

Charles took after his mother, Charlotte Fairchild, and long held dreams of following in her footsteps and serving as Consul. As a child, he would assist Charlotte in her work; bringing her papers, adjusting the witchlight, refilling her inkwell. Charles always wanted to talk politics as well, but Charlotte was careful to be discreet when he was around.

Charles Fairchild

Motherwort ♀ Concealed Love

Christopher Lightwood

Born 1887
Species Nephilim
Favorite weapon His own inventions
Family Lightwood, Herondale

Christopher Lightwood was lucky to find a mentor in his family's old friend, Henry Branwell. Henry's eccentricities paved the way for Christopher in their community; by the time Christopher came along, his parents and their friends were familiar with the ins and outs of life with a creative (yet absent-minded) genius. Though the Clave frowns on experimentation, Christopher's family supported his curiosity and innovation.

Christopher Lightwood

White-Pink Geranium 🐿 Ingenious Talent

Cordelia Carstairs

Born 1885
Species Nephilim
Favorite weapon Cortana
Family Carstairs, Turan

Cordelia has a mischievous streak. When she was growing up, she loved scaring her brother Alastair. Her favorite method was to hide under his bed and grab his ankle when he got close enough to reach. To this day, Alastair looks under beds before getting within arm's length of them.

Cordelia Carstairs

Daisy ✤ Loyal Love

Grace Blackthorn

Born 1886
Species Nephilim
Favorite weapon Hairpins
Family Cartwright, Blackthorn

Grace had one hobby she retained from before she was adopted by Tatiana Blackthorn. She would gather flowers, leaves, and vines, and twist them together into elaborate crowns. Her adoptive brother, Jesse Blackthorn, and Tatiana were not generally willing to wear crowns, so Grace kept most of them, hanging them on nails driven into the walls of her bedroom.

Grace Blackthorn

Hydrangea ✿ *Cold Heartlessness*

James Herondale

Born 1886
Species Nephilim
Favorite weapon Throwing knives
Family Herondale, Gray

S ome of James's fondest memories are of his parents, Will and Tessa Herondale, reading out loud to him and his sister Lucie. The four would read together almost every evening, snuggled onto the sofa in front of the hearth. James and Lucie took turns reading once they learned how.

Forget me Not ❈ True Love

Jesse Blackthorn

Born 1879
Species Nephilim
Favorite weapon Unknown
Family Blackthorn, Lightwood

Jesse Blackthorn was raised in isolation, with only his mother Tatiana and his sister, Grace, for company. In this bleak environment, Jesse had to find his own happiness wherever he could. Frequently confined to bed because of illness, Jesse perfected his own paper-folding and cutting technique, making plants and animals from scraps of newsprint.

Cyclamen ❧ Resignation

Lucie Herondale

Born 1887
Species Nephilim
Favorite weapon The pen
(mightier than the sword)
Family Herondale, Gray

L ucie loved writing ever since she could hold a pen. One of her prize possessions was a thick blank book that her brother, James Herondale, gave her for her eighth birthday. She kept it next to her bed, and copied only her favorite pieces of her own work into it. When Lucie was in her teens, she penned a novel titled *The Beautiful Cordelia* that reached a length of two thousand pages.

Lucie Herondale

Chrysanthemum 🌼 *Cheerful Under Adversity*

Matthew Fairchild

Born 1886
Species Nephilim
Favorite weapon Rapier
Family Fairchild, Branwell

Matthew was very close with his father, Henry Branwell, but this closeness was not always easy. Matthew found himself caring for his father; making sure Henry ate and slept and didn't set himself on fire. This responsibility was a heavy one for a young child, but Matthew handled it with determination. A core as solid as iron lay under his flamboyant nature.

Matthew Fairchild

Green Carnation ✦ *Love of what is Beautiful*

Sona Turan Carstairs

Born 1850
Species Nephilim
Married names Verlac, Carstairs
Favorite weapon Shamshir
Family Turan, Unknown

Born in Tehran, Sona was an only child who grew up accustomed to getting her way. After the death of her first husband, Theodor Verlac, she married Elias Carstairs, who refused to believe the rumors that Sona had poisoned Theodor.

Sona Carstairs

Gardenia ❧ Refinement

Thomas Lightwood

Born 1885
Species Nephilim
Favorite weapon Broadsword
Family Lightwood, Ashdown

Thomas Lightwood was unhealthy when he was a child. His concerned family kept a close eye on him—a little too close. Thomas craved solitude, and was frustrated by the constant attentions of his older sisters. One day when he was left unattended, Thomas found a hole in a crumbling wall in the garden. The opening, obscured behind an evergreen bush, led to the surrounding forest. Thereafter, when Thomas was in need of peace and quiet, he'd slip away and walk among the trees of Idris, composing songs and stories in his mind.

Thomas Lightwood

Red Catchfly ❦ Youthful Energy

The Mortal Instruments

Alexander Gideon Lightwood

Born 1989
Species Nephilim
Favorite weapon Bow and arrow
Family Lightwood, Trueblood

Alec's seemingly endless supply of faded, unraveling sweaters don't reflect his vibrant nature. His whimsical streak was apparent when he threw a surprise birthday party for Magnus Bane where the guests were almost exclusively cats, as a reversal of Magnus's own history of throwing elaborate birthday parties for Chairman Meow. Chairman Meow was not amused.

Alec Lightwood

Daphne ∽ Don't Change

Aline Blackthorn Penhallow

Born 1990
Species Nephilim
Maiden name Penhallow
Favorite weapon Blades
Family Penhallow, Ke

Making the best of a terrible situation, Aline picked up a new hobby early in her time on Wrangel Island: ice sculpture. Aline excels at the detail-oriented work, and uses a variety of weapons for carving. Her best known piece is her rendering of Jonathan Shadowhunter, carved entirely with seraph blade, but her favorite subject is her wife, Helen Blackthorn.

Aline Penhallow

Scarlet Zinnia ∽ Constancy

Amatis Herondale

Born 1967
Species Nephilim
Maiden name Graymark
Favorite weapon Short sword
Family Graymark, Unknown

When Amatis was a child, she often devised games to keep her younger brother, Lucian Graymark, entertained. A particular favorite was "Elphas and Baba," in which Amatis and Luke would pretend to be the ancient warlock siblings Baba Agnieszka and Elphas the Unsteady. The game generally involved Amatis (as Baba) ordering Luke to collect unusual objects to use as spell components. Occasionally when Luke was in a bad mood, Amatis would let him play Baba, and he delighted in making bizarre demands of his sister.

Amatis Graymark

Locust Tree l Love Beyond the Grave

Asmodeus

Born Unknown
Species Prince of Hell
Favorite weapon Unknown

As a Prince of Hell, Asmodeus has an insatiable hunger for the suffering of humans. Indeed, any sort of strong emotion feeds him. A sixteenth century seeress delivered a prophecy that his addiction to the emotions and memories of humans would be his undoing, but he remains unconcerned. Asmodeus isn't one to trouble himself with pathetic human superstition.

Asmodeus

Dragonwort ∽ Horror

Bartholomew Velasquez

Born 1988
Species Werewolf
Favorite weapon Wolf form

Bat Velasquez has an independent streak that makes him stand out among the werewolves of the New York pack. The majority of werewolves rely heavily on a pack for food, shelter, and emotional support, and give up most of the connections to their former lives. Bat has never been willing to give up his earlier lifestyle and passions. Rather than living with the pack, Bat has an apartment of his own. He has an active creative life as a DJ. His willingness to blaze a middle way through the dichotomy of human/werewolf has enabled him to make important contributions to the re-establishment of the Praetor Lupus.

Bat Velasquez

Helmet Flower ~ Chivalry

Brother Zachariah

Created 1878
Species Nephilim
Favorite weapon Staff
Family Carstairs, Ke

Joining the Silent Brothers is no easy task. There is a steep learning curve, especially in the first decade of service to the Brotherhood. While he struggled with his personal transformation, Brother Zachariah brought the gift of perspective to the other Silent Brothers. Isolated as they are, it had been decades since the Brothers had lived beside a Shadowhunter whose humanity remained so close. Brother Zachariah's presence reinvigorated the Brothers, reminding them of the preciousness of the life for which they study and fight.

Brother Zachariah

Zephyr ∽ Waiting

Camille Belcourt

Born Unknown
Species Vampire
Favorite weapon Manipulation

As an ancient vampire, Camille had many opportunities to reinvent herself. A little known chapter of her history was her ill-fated brush with millinery. In the early 1800s, Camille began designing extravagant hats. For vampires, she favored rich colors and jewels to contrast with their unnatural pallor. For werewolves, earth tones and striking textures were employed. Camille did not often have the opportunity to design for warlocks, but when she did she made reference to the magical specialties of her clients in the materials she chose. The hats she made for the fey often featured moss and enchanted, undying flowers. All of her hats had magic woven through them, and it was those enchantments that brought this chapter of her life to a sudden end. Quite a large number of the hats began to move of their own accord, and some became aggressive. No warlock has admitted to helping Camille create these unfortunate hats, and she has never revealed the identity of her magical helper... possibly because she enacted some horrible revenge upon them.

Camille Belcourt

Hortensia ❧ Cold-Hearted

Catarina Loss

Born Unknown
Species Warlock
Favorite weapon Unknown

atarina's specialty is healing magic. She has worked in a wide variety of medical settings in the mundane human world, from field hospitals in times of war to state-of-the-art clinics. In cases of extreme need, Catarina has even used portal magic to treat and extract earthquake victims, but the risk of using such magic is great. In general, Catarina prefers to hang back until her healing magic will count the most. Because of her involvement with mundane institutions, Catarina has expertise on navigating the mundane world that many individuals from the Shadow World lack. She's a great resource to mundane humans, Shadowhunters, and Downworlders alike.

Catarina Loss

Mullein ✽ Healing

Céline Herondale

Born 1971
Species Nephilim
Maiden name Montclaire
Favorite weapon Unknown
Family Montclaire, Unknown

Céline struggled with not belonging during her early life. She grew up in an abusive situation, with parents who treated her brutally and rarely showed her any kindness. As a child, Céline often ran away from home, sometimes staying away for days at a time. Though she was frequently hungry, those days of solitude were her rare moments of peace. In the many stressful moments of her life, she would recall those days spent walking in the forest or along roads, blissfully anonymous. She could be anyone, going anywhere. Before meeting Valentine Morgenstern and joining up with the Circle, Céline was considering continuing her path of solitude and becoming an Iron Sister, but after her hellish upbringing she chafed at the idea of the discipline required. The Circle gave her a place to belong without total isolation, where she had friends and comrades. She threw herself into their world, unaware of the devastating consequences her loyalty would have.

Céline Montclaire

Wisteria ❧ Regret

Chairman Meow

Born 2005
Species Cat
Favorite weapon Innate charm

The warlock Magnus Bane found Chairman Meow abandoned in an alley near his apartment building. Chairman Meow was in a dilapidated cardboard box along with three other kittens. After several days of four-kitten hijinks, Magnus cast a spell to determine which of his neighbors were most in need of a kitten, and dispersed the other three to some very surprised mundane humans. Chairman Meow made it clear he had no intention of leaving by clinging to Magnus any chance he got.

Chairman Meow

Angelica § Magic & Inspiration

Church

Born Unknown
Species Cat (rendered immortal
through necromantic
experiments)
Favorite weapon Teeth, claws,
withering glances

C hurch first came to Manhattan with the warlock Magnus Bane. While he did refrain from biting Magnus on the transatlantic voyage, he did suffer bouts of seasickness. If he had such capability, he probably would have chided Magnus about his frivolous decision to travel like a mundane "for fun." Possessing no such faculty for reason, Church merely treated Magnus to some long, vicious stares.

Church is currently retired and lives on the beach.

Church

Garland of Roses ∽ *Superior Merit*

Clary Adele Fray

Born 1991
Species Nephilim
Favorite weapon Short sword (Heosphoros)
Family Fairchild, Morgenstern

Clary Fray hasn't let her responsibilities as a Shadowhunter interfere with her artistic life. After the Dark War, Clary set up a studio space in an unused bedroom at the New York Institute, near the music room. She devotes several hours a week to drawing and painting, and sometimes her mother, Jocelyn Fray, joins her. Jace Herondale often uses those same hours to play the piano.

Clary was given her middle name, Adele, to honor her maternal grandmother, but the name has a long history among the Nephilim.

Clary Fray

Violets ∾ Loyalty

Helen Penhallow Blackthorn

Born 1989
Species Nephilim
Maiden name Blackthorn
Favorite weapon Seraph blade
Family Blackthorn

Banished to study the wards on Wrangel Island, Helen has struggled with the grief of being separated from her family. One saving grace is that she has developed a fascination with the wards themselves. Shadowhunters rely heavily on warding magic, but their understanding of it is relatively small. With Helen's determination and focus, she's on a path to become one of the foremost experts on wards. She hopes that this expertise will eventually entice the Nephilim to allow her to return home.

Helen Blackthorn

Helenium ∽ Tears

Hodge Starkweather

Born 1971
Species Nephilim
Favorite weapon Chakram
Family Starkweather, Unknown

T he Starkweather family has long favored isolation in the countryside of Idris. Hodge was often left to his own devices, and spent hours roaming the fields and forests. Plants and animals were of particular interest to him, and he became a skilled herbalist in his youth. Hodge had to go to great lengths to convince his parents to let him attend the Shadowhunter Academy, and when he did, it wasn't an easy place for him to be. Those years spent in the wilderness and the apothecary turned out to be some of his happiest memories.

Judas tree ✼ Betrayer

Imogen Herondale

Born 1946
Species Nephilim
Maiden name Whitelaw
Favorite weapon Seraph blade
Family Whitelaw, Unknown

Few individuals can claim to have seen the softer side of Imogen Herondale. Even before the tragic losses of her husband, son, and daughter-in-law, Imogen had a flinty personality. While impatient with nonsense and frivolous behavior, Imogen also had a surprising number of hobbies: watercolor painting, poison-mixing, darts, and classical piano.

Imogen Herondale

Coltsfoot & Justice Shall be Done

Isabelle Sophia Lightwood

Born 1991
Species Nephilim
Favorite weapon Whip
Family Lightwood, Trueblood

I sabelle Lightwood's nerdy tendencies began long before she formed a close relationship with Simon Lewis. As a young girl, Isabelle was fascinated by the history of weapons. She balanced the time she spent doing physical training with hours in the library, reading about the evolution and practice of close-range combat. While not always the most attentive student, Isabelle's attention to anything involving weapons was, to quote her former tutor Hodge Starkweather, "terrifying."

Isabelle Lightwood

Purple Columbine § Resolved to Win

Jace Herondale

Born 1991
Species Nephilim
Favorite weapon Blades
Family Herondale, Montclaire, Lightwood

Taking a page out of Clary Fray's book, Jace Herondale adopted a regular artistic practice. In between training and Institute business, Jace has turned more seriously to music, teaching himself challenging pieces and even composing original works. Despite a shared interest in music, Jace and Simon Lewis have only collaborated once, on a song titled *Come Back, Meow*, dedicated to Magnus Bane's cat.

§

Jace Herondale

Red Camellia ❧ Fire in my Heart

Jia Penhallow

Born 1967
Species Nephilim
Maiden name Ke
Favorite weapon Changdao
Family Ke, Wang

S erving as Consul is no easy task. Jia understands the importance of leisure time now more than ever, and has a carefully designed routine for de-stressing. Jia starts with a swim, the rigor of which is based on how difficult her day has been. Then she takes a leisurely walk in the hills around Idris or in the Penhallow garden, and wraps up the routine with a cup of hot chocolate and a novel to read. She also frequently writes letters to her daughter, Aline Blackthorn Penhallow, in the evenings.

Jocelyn Fray

Born 1970
Species Nephilim
Maiden name Fairchild
Favorite weapon Short sword
Family Fairchild, Nightshade

Once the danger of the Dark War passed, Jocelyn renewed her devotion to painting. Jocelyn's newer work has taken on a luminous quality, encompassing a mixture of joy and sorrow that has elevated her work from excellent to masterful. She credits the energy created by giving up her double life as the source of her inspiration.

Daylily ∽ Mother's Love

Jonathan Christopher Morgenstern

Born 1990
Species Nephilim
Favorite weapon Broadsword (Phaesphoros)
Family Morgenstern, Fairchild

In his youth, Jonathan Morgenstern was frequently left on his own. His father, Valentine Morgenstern, had a whole other life separate from Jonathan, complete with a second "son" who lived in Wayland Manor. Jonathan disliked being left alone, and his restlessness caused him to devise subtle tricks to play on Valentine. He routinely rearranged the papers on Valentine's desk, hid his favorite stele, and taught Hugin and Munin bad behaviors, such as taking people's hats off and tearing their clothes. Valentine, while annoyed, was secretly relieved that his son was not doing much, much worse.

Jonathan Morgenstern

Monkshood & Beware a Deadly Foe

Jonathan Fairchild Morgenstern

Born 1990
Species Nephilim
Favorite weapon Unknown
Family Morgenstern, Fairchild

J onathan Fairchild Morgenstern never had the chance to exist. He was a might-have-been, twisted into an unrecognizable shape by Valentine Morgenstern's experimentation before he was even born. Clary Fray had two glimpses of the brother she never had, once in a vision brought on by a demon, and once when heavenly fire burned out the evil in Jonathan. What was left was not enough to survive. While Jocelyn Fray and Clary could not mourn for the Jonathan they knew, they both mourned the person he could have been.

"True" Jonathan Morgenstern

Snowdrop ❦ Hope

Jonathan Shadowhunter

Born Unknown
Species Nephilim
Favorite weapon Unknown
Family Unknown

L ittle is known of Jonathan Shadowhunter's early life, yet we do know that he was close with his elder sister Abigail. When Jonathan encountered the angel Raziel and created the Nephilim, he was traveling with Abigail and his friend David. Abigail was on her way to meet the man she was betrothed to, and the angel episode diverted her from that path. Jonathan was delighted, for he preferred to have his sister close by. Historical records show that Jonathan frequently mentioned how pleased he was that Abigail remained by his side.

❧ ❦

Jonathan Shadowhunter

Nasturtium ❦❦❦ Patriotism

Jordan Kyle

Born 1989
Species Werewolf
Favorite weapon Wolf form

J ordan Kyle was killed by Jonathan Morgenstern along with the rest of the Praetor Lupus, but he did leave a musical legacy behind. Simon Lewis's final recording with his band, The Mortal Instruments, was an eleven minute track dedicated to Jordan. The band mixed parts of Jordan's demos into the song, though it was primarily instrumental. *Beati Bellicosi* is widely considered to be among their best work.

Jordan Kyle

Asphodel ✤ Regrets

Lily Chen

Born Unknown
Species Vampire
Favorite weapon Unknown

Lily's room at the Hotel Dumort is fastidiously decorated, in contrast to the shabby exterior, with a varnished wood floor and silk curtains. Lily prides herself on her decorating skills, and can often be found trying out new ideas in other rooms of the hotel. Some of the clan members appreciate this hobby more than others.

Lily Chen

Hollyhock ❖ Ambition

Luke Garroway

Born 1970
Species Werewolf
Favorite weapon Kindjal
Family Graymark

Luke may have been living a double life when he opened Garroway Books in Williamsburg, but his love of literature was no cover story. Luke was primarily raised by his older sister Amatis Graymark, after their mother left to become an Iron Sister. Life wasn't easy for the Graymark children, but books proved to be a refuge and an escape for Luke. One of his fondest dreams was to have his own bookstore someday.

Luke Garroway

Wolfsbane ❧ Knight

Magnus Bane

Born Unknown
Species Warlock
Favorite weapon Magic, devastating charm

After a streak of partying too hard in the 1970s, Magnus decided he needed to develop more introverted habits. He had a brief encounter with philately (stamp-collecting), but found all the sorting rather tedious. An interest in cultivating Bonsai trees followed, but was rather pointless for someone who could manipulate the size of plants at will. Realizing that he needed a more lively hobby, Magnus made a habit of throwing elaborate theme parties, an activity that suited him much better.

Magnus Bane

Acorn & Immortality

Maia Roberts

Born 1990
Species Werewolf
Favorite weapon Wolf form

Maia loves vinyl records. She has an extensive collection of albums, and makes time in her busy schedule of Praetor Lupus business to attend concerts and visit record stores. After re-establishing the Praetor Lupus, Maia got a second tattoo: a botanical illustration of the wolfsbane plant, Aconitum.

Werewolf business aside, Maia got her GED, and followed it with a degree in business studies from Brooklyn College. She's considering opening a nightclub with Bat Velasquez.

Maia Roberts

Gladiolus ❦ Strength of Character

Malcolm Fade

Born Unknown
Species Warlock
Favorite weapon Magic

L iving in Los Angeles, Malcolm has been unable to avoid occasional participation in the movie business. Usually hired by producers who crave a dash of true showbiz magic, the warlock has been known to become too invested in the storylines of films, relentlessly pushing for happy endings. He doesn't have many repeat clients.

Malcolm Fade

Witch Hazel & Spells

Maryse Lightwood

Born 1968
Species Nephilim
Maiden name Trueblood
Favorite weapon Broadsword
Family Trueblood, Unknown

Maryse was unusually short until she hit a dramatic growth spurt in her early teens. Young Maryse refused to let her stature limit the sort of weapons she would train with, but the broadsword evaded her. When she finally shot up, Maryse was delighted to be able to wield the giant weapon, and it has been a favorite of hers ever since.

Maryse Lightwood

Lotus ∞ Estranged Love

Maureen Brown

Born 1993
Species Vampire
Favorite weapon Teeth

When Maureen is spoken of, she is usually recalled as a vicious vampire queen. It is rarely acknowledged that before she was Turned, she had relatively ordinary hobbies: knitting, soccer, and playing the piano. She was also a Girl Scout, but was too shy to make much money from cookie sales.

Maureen Brown

Black Rose ∿ Obsession

Maxwell Joseph Lightwood

Born 1998
Species Nephilim
Favorite weapon Unknown
Family Lightwood, Trueblood

Before his untimely death, Max was an enthusiastic reader. While there are few children's books written for Shadowhunters, the New York Institute did have an extensive library of folk and fairy tales from around the world. Max devoured these eagerly. The tales of dark magic and beasts resonated with him, for he routinely watched his family go off to fight demons and face danger.

Max Lightwood

Harebell ~ Grief

Max Michael Lightwood-Bane

Born 2009
Species Warlock
Favorite weapon Unknown
Family Lightwood, Bane

Max enjoys books and playing with common household objects. The identities of his biological human parent and demon parent are unknown. He calls Alec "dad" and Magnus "papa." He wants to be a pirate.

Max Michael Lightwood-Bane

Lavender Rose ∞ Enchantment

Meliorn

Born Unknown
Species Half-human, half fey
Favorite weapon Deceit

As a half-human, Meliorn was not easily accepted by many of the fey. Despite living among them for over a hundred years, many faeries considered him an outsider. The Seelie Queen was one of his few true allies. From the time Meliorn was a child, she made it known that he had a place at her court, a position that granted him social standing he otherwise would not have held. He repaid her with his loyalty, to the last.

Meliorn

Straw ∞ Broken Contract

Michael Wayland

Born 1965
Species Nephilim
Favorite weapon Blades
Family Wayland, Unknown

After leaving the Shadowhunter Academy, Michael became fascinated by his lineage as a Wayland. He began to teach himself how to make weapons. This was an odd hobby for a Shadowhunter, for the Nephilim usually rely on the Iron Sisters to keep them armed. Michael's blades were no objects of beauty; they were crude but well balanced. Michael's forge still stands behind the wreckage of Wayland Manor.

Michael Wayland

Michaelmas Daisy ⁓ Farewell

Rafael Santiago Lightwood-Bane

Born 2007
Species Nephilim
Favorite weapon Unknown
Family Lightwood, Bane

Rafael loves music, especially lullabies in Spanish. He also enjoys dancing, hide and seek, and light-up sneakers. The identities of his birth parents are unknown.

Rafael Santiago Lightwood-Bane

Persicaria ∽ Restoration

Ragnor Fell

Born Unknown
Species Warlock
Favorite weapon Magic

After Ragnor's murder, few felt his absence as strongly as Catarina Loss. As warlocks, the two had known each other for a very long time. Catarina has a tendency to overwork, and Ragnor had a unique ability to convince her to take time off. On these spontaneous vacations, the two went hiking, visited hot springs and unusual geological formations. Occasionally they invited Magnus Bane along, but he didn't enjoy roughing it quite as much as they did.

Lemon Blossom ∽ Discretion

Raphael Santiago

Born 1937
Species Vampire
Favorite weapon Bite

Raphael was admired for his leadership of the New York vampire clan. When he was killed, the clan wanted to honor his memory. After much debate, it was decided that the best honor would be to contribute to the health of the East Harlem neighborhood that is the home of the Hotel Dumort, since Raphael had grown up nearby. The presence of nocturnal good samaritans picking up trash, shoveling snow, and making sure residents get home safe is occasionally remarked upon by the mundane neighbors.

Raphael Santiago

Hellebore ❀ Bitter Memories

Raziel

Born Unknown
Species Angel
Favorite weapon Unknown

L ittle is known of Raziel, as befits the Angel of Secrets.

Raziel

Fleur de Lis ❦ Flame of Power

Robert Lightwood

Born 1965
Species Nephilim
Favorite weapon Broadsword
Family Lightwood, Gladstone

When Robert and Maryse Lightwood were banished to the New York Institute, they went through a period of shock and mourning. The disaster that was the Uprising and their subsequent departure from Idris left them reeling. Robert found comfort in a surprisingly tender activity: reading aloud to his children. Alec Lightwood was two years old, and Isabelle Lightwood only a baby, but Robert spent hours reading aloud to them from classic novels, history books, and even Clave documents.

Robert Lightwood

Jasmine ❧ Separation

Seelie Queen

Born Unknown
Species Fey
Favorite weapon The desires of human hearts

The Seelie Queen keeps the details of her past closely guarded from mortals, vampires, and warlocks alike. She is famously cruel, but there have been times when she has shown something resembling kindness. When the half-faerie Meliorn was brought to her court, there were those who mocked him for his human blood. The Queen was not one of them. She treated him as a full faerie– better, even— and swiftly punished any who treated him unfairly.

Seelie Queen

Dog Rose ❧ Pleasure & Pain

Simon Lewis

Born 1990
Species Nephilim (Ascendant)
Favorite weapon Bow and arrow

When Simon became a Shadowhunter, he wanted to find ways to keep in touch with his family that would not involve sharing too many details of his life. He and his sister Rebecca Lewis found a creative way to communicate: they're collaborating on an epic, exquisite-corpse style manuscript, alternating sentences via text message. The story involves space travel, warring kingdoms, and many types of aliens. Honestly, it's really hard to follow.

Geranium / True Friendship

Stephen William Herondale

Born 1966
Species Nephilim
Favorite weapon Longsword
Family Herondale, Whitelaw

When Stephen was a child, he was fond of quilting. He had learned the skill from his grandmother, Arabella Whitelaw. Imogen Herondale did not get along with her mother. Jealous of Arabella's closeness with her son, Imogen cruelly mocked him for the hobby. After Arabella died, Stephen gave up quilting… where anyone could see. Amatis Herondale, Stephen's ex-wife, admitting to seeing him take a few stitches when he needed to unwind after a long day.

Stephen Herondale

Evening Primrose & Unfaithfulness

The Band: Eric, Kirk & Matt

Born 1990
Species Mundane human
Favorite weapon Terrible lyrics

T he Mortal Instruments (as they are now known) are alternately celebrated and scolded for their wild antics onstage. Elaborate costumes, fireworks, and dry ice are employed, as well as giant puppets and olfactory components. "It isn't just a show," says frontman Eric Hillchurch, "It's a full sensory experience."

Eric & Kirk & Matt

Reeds ♾ Music

Valentine Morgenstern

Born 1968
Species Nephilim
Favorite weapon Manipulation
Family Morgenstern, Unknown

When he was young, Valentine Morgenstern distinguished himself with an unusual skill for carving. His masterpiece, created at age fourteen, was a chess set carved from bone and horn. He wouldn't say where he got the raw materials. He gave up the craft soon after.

Valentine Morgenstern

Anemone ❧ Forsaken

Tales from the Shadowhunter Academy

Beatriz Velez Mendoza

Born 1991
Species Nephilim
Favorite weapon Seraph blade
Family Mendoza, Velez

When Beatriz was young, she overcame a debilitating fear of heights and went on to excel at rock climbing. This early triumph gifted her with the determination that has enabled her to become a highly skilled Shadowhunter.

Beatriz Velez Mendoza

Protea ❦ Learning

George Lovelace

Born 1990
Species Mundane human
Favorite weapon Staff
Family Lovelace (lapsed)

Growing up on a farm, George was no stranger to hard work. The physical labor he engaged in gave him plenty of time to daydream, and he often did, imagining a more adventurous life for himself. He shared some of these daydreams with his grandmother, who claimed to have had encounters with faeries. She encouraged him to write his daydreams down, turn them into stories, but doing so did not satisfy George. He wanted the stories to be real. Being offered the chance to attend the Shadowhunter Academy was quite literally a dream come true.

George Lovelace

Strawberry ∽ Future Promise

Tobias Herondale

Born Unknown
Species Nephilim (exiled)
Favorite weapon n/a
Family Herondale, Unknown

Tobias Herondale had too gentle of a soul to make a good Shadowhunter. As a child, his parents were deeply concerned about his mild nature, and pushed him to harden himself. Their challenges had the opposite effect; the more they leaned on him to behave as befits a warrior, the more passive he became. This cycle set the stage for his eventual disgrace.

Tobias Herondale

Pennyroyal ~ Flee Away

The Dark Artifices

Arthur Blackthorn

Born 1973
Species Nephilim
Favorite weapon Dagger
Family Blackthorn, Unknown

When Arthur lived in London, he conducted research at the city's many museums. He went so far as to befriend several mundane curators in order to gain access to collections that were not ordinarily open to the public. Arthur could be unexpectedly charming, when he felt his work depended on it.

Arthur Blackthorn

Ranunculus ⚜ Madness

Cameron Ashdown

Born 1994
Species Nephilim
Favorite weapon Seraph blade
Family Ashdown, Unknown

Cameron Ashdown took an unusual interest in mundane sports, his favorite being soccer. He and Emma often went running together while they were dating, ostensibly to be fit for training. Unbeknownst to Emma and his family, Cameron was hoping to join a local soccer club.

Cameron Ashdown

Daffodil 🌼 *Return my Affection*

Cristina Mendoza Rosales

Born 1994
Species Nephilim
Favorite weapon Balisong
Family Rosales, Mendoza

Cristina loved the gardens at the Mexico City Institute. In her early teens, she took to setting up targets so that she could practice throwing knives among the plants and shrubs. After she and Jaime Rosales frightened several visiting Shadowhunters, Cristina had to admit that knife-throwing and relaxing gardens are better kept separate.

Cristina Mendoza Rosales

Pink Morning Glory ❀ My Hopes Destroyed

Diana Wrayburn

Born 1985
Species Nephilim
Favorite weapon Throwing star
Family Wrayburn, Unknown

Diana spent many years in Thailand. She travelled Southeast Asia extensively, sometimes fighting demons and other times just soaking in the sensory experience of her journey. She made a point of visiting Angkor Wat, as well as many other sites of historical and spiritual importance.

Diana Wrayburn

Ivy 🌾 Endurance & Faith

Diego Rocío Rosales

Born 1993
Species Nephilim
Favorite weapon Axe
Family Rosales, Rocío

D iego's favorite meal is breakfast. When he was growing up, he would periodically get up before the rest of his family and surprise them with chilaquiles. He's equally enthusiastic about having breakfast for dinner.

Ginger Flower 🌼 I Have my Pride

Drusilla Blackthorn

Born 1999
Species Nephilim
Favorite weapon Unknown
Family Blackthorn, Unknown

Drusilla's brother Tiberius Blackthorn has a fascination with Sherlock Holmes, but Drusilla herself went through a detective phase as well. Emma Carstairs brought a box of Nancy Drew books home from a junk shop, and Drusilla made short work of them. "Sometimes it's nice to read an adventure story without any demons," she observed.

Drusilla Blackthorn

Purple Tulip 🌷 Daydreaming

Emma Cordelia Carstairs

Born 1995
Species Nephilim
Favorite weapon Cortana
Family Carstairs, Townsend

When Emma moved in with the Blackthorns at age twelve, she felt she had to create her own niche within the family. In between intensive training sessions, Emma would ride her bike to rummage sales and antique stores, picking up odd knick-knacks and toys, old books and magazines to share with the Blackthorn children.

Emma Carstairs

Hyacinth ❀ *My Heart in Battle*

Gwyn ap Nudd

Born Unknown
Species Fey
Favorite weapon Unknown

Gwyn commands the Wild Hunt. While he lives closely with his warriors, he maintains a degree of remove from them. His motivations and intentions are mysterious, even to the faerie courts.

Gwyn ap Nudd

Fir 🜊 Time Has No Meaning

Jaime Rocío Rosales

Born 1995
Species Nephilim
Favorite weapon Poison
Family Rosales, Rocío

J aime has a restless and mischievous spirit. He plays devil's advocate in arguments, a fact that Cristina Rosales, who once planned to be his parabatai, grudgingly accepted. Jaime often disappears for long periods without saying where he's going.

Jaime Rosales

Purple Carnation ❁ *Changeable Moods*

Johnny Rook

Born Unknown
Species Unknown
Favorite weapon Sorcery

J ohnny Rook has had a booth at the Shadow
Market since he was a teenager. At first the
denizens of the market dismissed him as a young,
foolish mundane, but Johnny's determination
and uncanny knack for gathering information soon
won him a respected place among their number.

Johnny Rook

Mock Orange ✿ Deceit

Julian Atticus Blackthorn

Born 1995
Species Nephilim
Favorite weapon Crossbow
Family Blackthorn, Unknown

The Blackthorn children generally respect that their older brother Julian needs time to paint. Their mother, a painter and photographer, emphasized the importance of creative work, and while they lost her early in their lives, her influence has shaped the family. Julian carries on her ideas about creativity beyond his own painting. He encourages his siblings to pursue their own individual interests, helping them in any way he can.

Julian Blackthorn

Auricula ✿ *I Paint My Heart*

Kieran

Born Unknown
Species Fey
Favorite weapon Unknown

Kieran's past is mysterious, and is rarely spoken of outside the Courts. He is one of the youngest and least regarded of the Unseelie King's fifty sons. Because of machinations behind the throne, Kieran was traded to the Wild Hunt at a young age.

Kieran

Yellow Rainflower ✤ *The Heart's Betrayal*

Lady Midnight

Born Unknown
Species Nephilim
Favorite weapon Unknown

Little is known of Lady Midnight. She is a phantom, not so much a person as a folkloric idea from a frightening story told to Shadowhunter children.

Black Tulip 🌷 Hopelessness

Livia Blackthorn

Born 1997
Species Nephilim
Favorite weapon Saber
Family Blackthorn, Unknown

Of all the Blackthorn siblings, Livvy is the most mathematically minded. Her siblings turn to her when they struggle with math, and she helps her brother Tiberius with the mathematical aspect of coding. Livia is fascinated by fractal patterns. The Blackthorn's tutor, Diana Wrayburn, occasionally finds herself wishing that Livia could have the opportunity to attend college and study higher level math.

Livia Blackthorn

Striped Rose 🌸 I hope for Unity

Mark Antony Blackthorn

Born 1991
Species Nephilim
Favorite weapon Elf bolt
Family Blackthorn

When he was ten years old, Mark Blackthorn was the resident pillow fort expert of the Los Angeles Institute. Many rainy days found Mark, the younger Blackthorns, and Emma Carstairs scouring the building for blankets and cushions, which they then rigged up into elaborate structures under Mark's supervision. Mark's older sister, Helen Blackthorn, could sometimes be convinced to join in as well.

Mark Blackthorn

Rose Leaves ✳ *Please Believe Me*

Octavian Blackthorn

Born 2004
Species Nephilim
Favorite weapon Unknown
Family Blackthorn, Unknown

There is a significant age gap between Octavian and his siblings, with Drusilla Blackthorn closest at five years his senior. This distance has encouraged him to cultivate his imagination and ability to entertain himself. Even when he was small, Octavian was frequently content to play by himself. He learned to read when he was only four, and mutual love of reading strengthened his connection with Drusilla.

Octavian Blackthorn

White Carnation 🐾 Innocence

Tiberius Nero Blackthorn

Born 1997
Species Nephilim
Favorite weapon Quarterstaff
Family Blackthorn, Unknown

Tiberius has always been fond of bees. While not as artistically inclined as his older brother Julian Blackthorn, Tiberius has been able to draw surprisingly realistic insects since he was young. He's especially proud of the ones that look real out of the corner of the observer's eye. He's managed to startle even his own siblings with them.

Tiberius Blackthorn

Thorn Apple 🌷 *My Heart Concealed by Thorns*